SILLY GRAMMAR STORY SERIES

FROWNS

NOUNS, A FEW ADJECTIVES

Words: Darcy Pattison

Art: John Joven

Frowns: Nouns, a Few Adjectives
by Darcy Pattison, illustrated by John Joven

Publisher's Cataloging-in-Publication Data

Names: Pattison, Darcy, author. | Joven, John, illustrator.
Title: Frowns : nouns , a few adjectives / by Darcy Pattison, illustrated by John Joven.
Series: Silly Grammar Story
Description: Little Rock, AR: Mims House, 2026. |
Summary: FROWNS reminds us that simple nouns hold power. In this verb-free picture book, a nervous new kid discovers that friendship can bloom—one noun at a time.
Identifiers: LCCN: 2026901498 | ISBN: 9781629443393 (hardcover) | 9781629443409 (paperback) | 9781629443416 (ebook) | 978-1-62944-342-3 (audio)
Subjects: LCSH Parts of speech--Juvenile fiction. | English language--Juvenile fiction. | English language--Noun--Juvenile fiction. | Friendship--Juvenile fiction. | BISAC JUVENILE FICTION / Concepts / Language | JUVENILE FICTION / Friendship
Classification: LCC PZ7.1 .P388 Fr 2026 | DDC [E]--dc23

NOTE: A noun is the name of a person, place or thing. In this book, persons/people are in purple. Places are in orange. Things are in blue. An adjective tells something more about a noun. Adjectives and punctuation are in black. Verbs, or action words—which shouldn't be in this book!—are in pink.

Frown.

Long,

long

hall.

A step.

A step.

Smaller steps.

Smallest steps.

Tall,

tall

door.

New kid.

Frown.

Ape

Kids!

6 glasses,
2 striped shirts,
3 backpacks,
many frowns.
Many, many frowns.

19 frowns!

2 smiles—
1 teacher, 1 kid.

Smile, striped shirt, glasses.

Bo!

Bo

Science!

Head bone.
Rib bones.
Leg bones.
Clean paper,
messy paper.

Bones
Bo

circle
triangle

Math!
Lines.
Sides.
Shapes.
Clean paper,
messy paper.

Lunchroom!

Clean hands, messy hands.

Playground!

Ladders, slides, ladders, slides.

Small smile.

Soccer field!

Bigger smile.
Kick.
Race.
Kick.
A tweet!

VERBS?

NO VERBS!

RED CARD!

VERBS!

GO!

Spelling!

F-r-e-n. F-r-e-n-d.

Better **speller**!

High fives.

Biggest smiles.

Bell!
Backpacks.
Car line.
Cars.
Cars.
Cars.

Frown! Cars?

"Mom!"

"Good day?"

Friends.
Smiles.

www.ingramcontent.com/pod-product-compliance
Lightning Source LLC
Chambersburg PA
CBHW042313170826
50016CB00011B/57
9781629443393